Copyright © 2019 by Adrianne Jones

All rights reserved. This book or any portion thereof may not be reproduced or used in any manner whatsoever without the express written permission of the publisher except for the use of brief quotations in a book review or scholarly journal.

First Edition: 2019

ISBN: 978-1-7923-2052-1

YAH-Scribe Publishing, LLC
21627 E. 9 Mile
Saint Clair Shores, MI 48080
hello@yahscribe.com
www.yahscribe.com

Light In The Darkness

ADRIANNE JONES

In the midst of Darkness you are unable to see what is before you. BUT there's always light at the end of the tunnel. But the LIGHT in the Darkness, shine so bright. I am loved by the Lord. I am thankful for you know me and still love me. I cannot earn your love it is freely given.

Acknowledgments

First and foremost all glory to God!!!

I would like to thank all who poured into me at any point in my life. My mother and father who is in Heaven, gone but not forgotten. My aunt Robinelle Pierce, my brother Julian Jordan,cousin/friend/sister Rekeshia Jones, my spirit mom (God chosen) Pamela Coleman, my mentor Tangie Yerger, Kirlene Roberts, Derin Moe Gray, Jazmin Cheatham, my daughter Ayana Dabo. Pastor Jim Heidrick and the whole Global Awakening School , as you prayed for me believed in me I thank you so much. Also The Rock City Heights Diiiiip family. Special thank you to Miguel Martinez for capturing the moments in the photos for the cover and the back cover.thank you all I appreciate each and every one who has been in my life for one reason, one season, one meaning.. 🩶

"Forget the former things; do not dwell on the past. See, I am doing a new thing! Now it springs up; do you not perceive it?
I am making a way in the wilderness and streams in the wasteland.

Isaiah 43:18-19

Table of Content

Night Terror	8
Secrets	9
Empty Spaces	11
Still	13
Expiration Date on Heartache	14
Forbidden Love	16
Hot & Cold	17
Rejection 1.0	20
Rejection 2.0	22
Picture perfect	24
Shattered Dreams	26
Flatline	29
Don't settle	32
Day Light	34
In The Mirror	35
Heartbeat	38
Thankful	40
Love / Obsession	43
True Love	45

A young girl being molested in the middle of the night. Confused, broken, and shame all hits her. The underlined question why me?..

Night Terror

Sleep interrupted

Giggle at my door

My body turns tense

Just like a thief in the night

You stole my innocence

Un-remorseful

Careless

I lay with shame

Confused

Brokenness

Secrets

Do you have secrets?

Family secrets?

Ok, how about things I rather not talk about

Better yet think about

Don't discuss outside of this house

Did you place that so deep down with in your soul

To the point only an X-Ray can reveal it?

Angry

Bitter

Pain

Sorrow

All oozing out of you

In Darkness secrets hide in places where the enemy lives

Open the blinds let the light come in

Let God's will heal you

His love is so sweet it's like a honeycomb

Honey overflows onto his people

Walk in his presence

Loneliness leads to calling someone in the past yet they keep popping up in the present. Looking for someone to fill a void. After a night of looking for the message in the bottle, leads to making that call to someone familiar. Only to realize they didn't fill the void for that long. Another piece broke

Empty Spaces

I look at the clock

I pick up the phone

I don't want to call

It's too late

A deep voice says hello

I say hi

I look at the wall

I look at the bed

You're next to me

I shake my head

One more call

One more kiss

One more rub

Hours of bliss

Years of sorrow

Temporary fulfillment

Lifetime of emptiness

Still

Still cross my mind

Still think of you

Still want you

Still love you

Still

Expiration Date on a Heartache

God I trust in you
I know you have a plan on my life
Your word says I have a plan to prosper you not to harm you
Then why does this hurt so bad
Clearly he has moved on why can't I?
How long am I suppose to mourn
Suppression leads to depression
I don't have time
But God she been dead for so many years I almost lost count

But why do I still think of her
Old bend up feelings recurring
Like backed child support
They coming to collect
Without warning
Leaves me speechless
Eyes are red
I can't sleep
Yet the outside thinks I'm

Growing and glowing
If they only knew behind the smile
A heartache I can no longer deny

Forbidden love

Forbidden: Not allowed

Unauthorized

Banned

Forbidden love

Eyes I've seen before

Our eyes meet like they never left

Scent I've smelt before

Love I've once knew

A touch I felt before

So long ago

A hug that intertwined our souls

How the grass is always greener

On the other side of the street

Tea is always sweeter

From someone else's cup

Hot & Cold

Uncontrollable

Our eyes met

Bodies are hot

But your heart is cold

I begin to turn

You had me in a hold

Entangled in your love

Then irruptedly it stops

No warning

No clue

Why you left me blue

Just like a rollercoaster

High

Low

Stop

I was on the right track

Shouldn't have looked back

Have you ever dated someone, maybe had an interest in someone just to be shut down. Ok, how about how about school application denied. Better yet unconditional love from parent; Mother's love undeniable, protection over their child like a lioness and her cub. A fathers love to provide protect and guide. So little boys know how to be a man and little girls know what to look for in a man. What if that love wasn't unconditional, there were conditions or no love at all...

Rejection 1.0

I look at you wide eye

You smile

I smile

We laugh

A nice greet until next time

We meet

Images in my mind of your desire

What it would be like to

Have you by my side

Thoughts of you in my mind

Visions of you in my eyes

Only to reveal its not me

I sit back comparing myself to this/that

Look in the mirror i don't see anything but lack

Big eyes

Big

Lips

Hips are curved

I'm far from thin

But i'm happy in my skin

Right?...

You walk in glowing like a light

Holding hands with another

Looked right passed me

As rejection reached out and snatched me

Rejection 2.0

I wish i never had you

I never asked to be here

You mad at me because I

Remind you of a night of fun

That lead to you having

Plus one

Pure pain in your eyes

Who hurt you; I thought

Failed at your own fantasies

Pride or protection

Unconditional love

Nonexistent

Strength or sorrow

Affection or abandon

Hugs or head nods

Smiles or glares

Love or look-a-like

Mother's bond.. Right?

You and the pipe were so tight

No need to chase it

You walked out

Raw rejection as I watched the door closed

Looked at the window, you never looked back

Picture Perfect

Just like a Polaroid picture smile

Twinkle in the eye or holding back tears

Faith it or fake it

I don't know the difference

Love or lust

Same thing right?

It's so perverse

Single and saved

Married and still looking

Or divorced and still together

Looking good or being good

Does it matter

Confident in promises

Delayed or denied

I'm so confused

I can't see my hand in front of my face

Yet I'm reaching for your grace

The picture I have made before you

Isn't the picture I see in the mirror

Shattered Dreams

The bible says 2 become 1

What if i have ½

You have ½

Is that still 1.?

Shattered pictures of a family

that no longer exists

Love no more

Broken pieces

I pick up slowly

Putting together the picture

I desperately want to have

Here we are broken

Looking for the pieces of the puzzle

To make it picture perfect

Picture broken

Just like us

No happily ever after

Losing a parent is one of the hardest things to experience at any age. An adult yet that little child lives inside scared and confused how could this be reality. This must be a dream of some short. Then to make matters worse you don't have the best relationship with that parent.

Flatline

How could you leave

With me having all these

unanswered questions

Full of rage,

resentment,

bitter

There you are flatline

They say forgive

Let it go

I guess this doesn't change anything

You've walked out when I was child

Physically that is

Now you'll never come back

How could you

I'll just keep calling your phone

Hoping you will pick up

Calls go unanswered

It wasn't until they closed the casket

That I'll never get the answer

Get to a point where you know you're worth! Don't go for second best in any situation. You deserve the upmost best in your life. Don't be afraid of the unknown. Be confident there's a plan for you in your life. The best is yet to come!

Don't Settle

Like a fork in the road

I don't know which way to turn

Stick with the comfort

Or wait on the unknown

The job promotion that the manager says no to

The business plan without the plan

The house the keys seem unreachable

The spouse that seems unreal to have

The car that the bank says no to

The baby that the doctor says it's impossible

Don't settle for the NO

Disappointment

Job promotion be the CEO

Business plan be in Forbes

Grab the keys to the House

Wait on the Spouse

Have the baby even if you have to wait until ninety!

Day Light

Bright eye

Brusy Tail

Golden skin

Confidence pours out of me

Joy in my smile

You tried to break me

But I stand boldly

Walk with a purpose

I have the victory

God didn't make no mistake on me

In the Mirror

Big eyes

Big lips

One dimple

One mold

Bold with gorgeous skin

Perfectly Imperfect

Love who I see in the mirror

Long hair

Short hair

I don't care

Curves that walk with their own rhythm

Music that has no beat

A song with no words

You walk with authority

You speak with boldness and confidence

Yet gentle and meek

Grace in thought

Compassion in heart

Empathy in action

Love and firmness in every motion

She is beautifully flawless

Glowing in confidence

I love her

I am her

The woman in the mirror

The joy of having a baby is so overwhelming! Most women want it more than anything. What about the sorrow of coming home with an empty car seat. The heartache of being a childless mother.

Heartbeat

Two Lines

one

Two heartbeats

One body

The joy of having you inside of me

The glory of life

Unexplainable

stomach growing

Can't see my feet

Water leaking

No warning

No little feet

Just like that

Back to one heartbeat

A letter to my daughter. The love I have for this child that grew inside of me. Day to day I am thankful God have you to me.

Thankful

Watching you sleep

Speechless

How did i get so blessed

Beautiful eyes

Eyes that look right through

They look right pass you

Look up to God

Knew this was from you

Brown skin

Heart of Gold

From the moment i saw you

I knew i would do everything for you

Your steps are guided

I wonder what's before you

What' love

Love is everything i lost

Everything i imagined

Wrapped in one

Love is you

I love you Ayana

After everything I been through this far you never left my side. In my imperfections you gave me mercy and love. In my weakness you gave me strength. In my fear you gave me faith. I was timid you turned me bold. I can't express how grateful I am, but I am determined to chase after you all the days of my life. As for me and my house will serve the Lord (Joshua 24:15)

Love/Obsession

Love

Definition: an intense feeling of deep affection

Obsession

Definition: the state of being obsessed with someone or something

An idea or thought that continually preoccupies pr intrudes on a person's mind

It started with infatuation

I want to see you

I want to hear you

I want to know you

I want to feel you

My devotion for you was borderline obsession

I knew it

I can't deny it

I don't want to fight it

I enjoyed it

Fixated on your sight

Addicted to your words

One word from you last a lifetime

Your presence is captivating

Here is where i want to be

Never leave

Passionate with your love

You invade my thoughts

I'm obsessed with my true love

My true love

Protects me

Guides me

Adores me

Fills me up

Restores me

When i am low

You lift me high

When all i see is dark

You shine the light

Feel you

Sense you

You're near

Concerned with my needs

I crave your tenderness

My devotion is all i have

I adore you my amor

Real Testimonies, real people from ones I know and love dearly including myself.

N.B

2003: Son told police he saw me cooking crack cocaine & child protective service nearly took my children.

January 13, 2004: Shot point blank range by a teenage friend.

August 2004: An eighteen-year-old girl was selling her body for me, escorting

March 4, 2005: Suicide attempt via drug overdose ecstasy and powder cocaine & contemplated blowing my brains out due to the change of life from being shot.

March 5, 2005: Sentence to nearly twenty years in Federal prison for state to state drug trafficking as a career offender

November 20, 2005: Notified by my wife that she was pregnant by another man.

September 2009: Wife divorced me and remarried.

April 9, 2018: Childhood friend stole nearly $100,000 dollars from me.

November 2018: Notified that my son contracted HIV.

When asked to write a testimony about my life, it gave me a chance to reflect over all that God has brought me through thus far. I remember going to God during my time of incarceration and saying to God, "If you want me to serve you, I need to know you beyond religion, culture, ethnicity, and what my mom or preachers says about you". "Or, how else will I know that you are real and the true God for me." This was important for me, because I had never met the 12 disciples, Paul, nor the people spoken about in the bible. I had been doing a life of crime, in-and-out of prison since I was a teenager. The only thing that I heard or knew about God is the fact that He was not while & Christianity was a white man's religion.

I've always had the call of God on my life. My mother has been in ministry to nearly 30 years, and even though she always tried to get me to "Stop running from the call of God on my life" I could not seem to adhere to her advice and wisdom at the time. You see, my knowledge about God was limited and honestly sin was pleasurable for me at the time. To make matter worse I was indoctrinated and influenced by the street life culture. I was deeply wrapped up in gangs, pimping, and drug selling. I had five children by four different women, no male figure to look up to, and my mother was doing the best she could as a single mother.

My father had been murdered by his wife, when I was a teenager. I believe he was a good man, but I knew very little about him. He lived I San Jose, California, and it was not until I was almost ten that my father and I met. However, it was not until I reached my forties that I learned the truth about my father and the truth about the history of how I ended up with my stepfather's last name.

Today as a free man I enjoy the liberty that has been found in Christ Jesus. People said that, "Due to my felony I'll never be able to get a good job". Currently, I work for Covance one the largest pharmaceutical staffing companies. God told me, while I was in prison that "If I was willing to allow Him to use me to minister to the hurting men in prison I will never have to look back". God has held true to that promise. I've received 2 promotions within the last 8 months that has put me on the fast track to becoming a supervisor; I'm functioning in the advancing the kingdom of God, I have healthier friendships; now that my heart has healed I'm dating and open to being in love again; I'm in the process of getting my business Noble Worldwide Investment underway; and God has given me favor in places that I never expected favor before.

The journey of life with God has been interesting, while simultaneously rewarding. Just being open to what He wants for my life has transformed me into a new man full of His love and grace. I learned a long time ago that "No test....No testimony".

Adrianne

10 years old –-18 years old (1996-2004)

My mom got involved with drugs heavily. In this time period she was also diagnosed with Bipolar Disorder. There was abuse in the household of every kind constantly walking on eggshells. At times we were homeless, sleeping in hotels or even the car. When I was 15 my mom left us (my brother and myself) we stayed with my stepdad. Once I turn 18 I moved out on my own and never looked back.

18-26 years old (2004-2012)

I had always worked Professionally looked the part. Daily looked for the answer of my problem in the bottle. Drinking daily. Had a miscarriage. Got married had an amazing job and baby! Things looked picture perfect right? Not so. A blessing too soon is a curse. 2 broken people don't make you whole. Got a divorce, lost my job now who was I? A mother to a child that I had no idea how to be a mother to.

27-32 (2012-2019)

My mom and dad passed away within 6 months apart. I had so much resentment for my mom not being there in my life the way I thought she should of been, she met my daughter at the age of 2 on her deathbed in the hospital. Suppressing my feelings was easy. Hiding what I'm going through and wearing a smile but hurting inside was so normal I was numb to the pain. I started going to a church revived church hurt and was lost in life completely at rock bottom. Thoughts of suicide was so realistic in my mind. I didn't know which way to go. I received a message from a lady I never met before who prayed against suicide, never told anyone my thoughts because of shame.

Responded to her message. At thought moment I felt Gods presence he reached his hand out and touched making a way in my life where I saw no way. I changed churches, had to move due to where I was living my roommate told me come back to church or move out per leadership. So I moved had no where to go, a lady allowed me to stay at her place. As I was looking for a place permanently for me and my daughter I received a call for a job I wasn't applying for jobs. Wasn't getting approved for a place either didn't make enough money. Went on this job interview got the job an increase financially immediately. A couple weeks later got a place. Months later a new car. Serving in a church growing and glowing. Falling and getting back up. He made a way when I was ready to give up on everything.

These are a few testimonies in my story more happened more to come. My story isn't over but it still going. These hurdles didn't kill me. I'm still standing. I'm overcomer. I don't know your story but I know God has a plan on your life . No matter what happens, how many times something bad happens, how many times you mess up. HIS word will NOT return VOLD. Hold on to the promises

Thank you all for taking the time to read my book. Each poem is my testimony one part in my life. I poured my heart into these poems. I pray that you were touched by this book. Know this whatever comes your way will not break you instead mold you for what's to come through you!

www.ingramcontent.com/pod-product-compliance
Ingram Content Group UK Ltd.
Pitfield, Milton Keynes, MK11 3LW, UK
UKHW041956230426
12048UKWH00008B/377